The Wild Essential

The Wild Essential

Poems by

Claudine Nash

Kelsay Books

Cover art: *Dandelions* by Carlos Monteagudo

ISBN: 13-978-1-947465-19-0

Kelsay Books
Aldrich Press
www.kelsaybooks.com

For My Lovely Ella

Acknowledgments

Many thanks and much appreciation to the editors of the following publications where these poems previously appeared:

82 Review: "As I Brew My Morning Coffee"
BlazeVOX: "Anatomy of a Moment" and "I Keep Checking My Samsung Galaxy for Meaning"
Indiana Voice Journal: "Warm Your One Sure Purpose"
Lady Chaos Press - Headlines and Tragedies Anthology: "Headline News"
Madness Muse Magazine: "Mind Monkeys"
Peacock Journal: "Blue Moon," "Now and Here," "Why I Received a Needs Improvement on My Last Employee Evaluation," and "Sometimes When It Storms"
Peaking Cat Poetry Magazine: "Backwoods" and "Morning Blend"
Sick Lit Magazine: "An Open Letter to My True Self," "Make a Moment," "Oxytocin," "Unbecoming," and "You Might Have Saved a Life Tonight"
Scarlet Leaf Review: "How to Come Full Circle in Five Steps, More or Less," "To the Moon," and "A Kinder Suit"
The Compassion Anthology: "After Cloud Cover"
The Icarus Anthology: "Lost and Found"
The Poeming Pigeon - Poems from the Garden: "A Beautiful Rain"
Thirty West Publishing House: "Songbird"
Transcendent Zero Press Selfhood Anthology: "Silence is the New Black"
Waxing and Waning: A Literary Journal: "Free as a Bear," "I Carry a Field," "The Wild Essential" "Watermarks" and "Your Biggest Thought"
Yellow Chair Review: "You are a Mountain" and "Magnolias"

"Blue Moon" was inspired by an NPR *On Being* interview given by the late John O'Donohue.

"As I Brew My Morning Coffee" was inspired by my daughter Ella Hackney who has asked me a version of almost every one of those questions, most of which during my pre-caffeinated state.

Much love and gratitude to Stanley Nash, Karen Nash, The Petricca Family, Dale Katz, Carlos Monteagudo, Jennifer Padrone, Scott Plous, Sheryl Rubin and to the regulars at the For the Love of Words open mic nights for their incredible support and encouragement, both past and present. Extra special thanks to Chris and Ella Hackney for sharing me with my laptop.

Contents

III

Somewhere, something incredible is waiting to be known.

—Carl Sagan

I.

You Are a Mountain

A river rock sits in you,
no, a rock face, no,
a mountain, yes

a thick, unyielding
mountain rises from
a solid place
within you.

Its foothills spread
into the corners where
your doubts take root

then dislodge, no,
displace, no,

tear, yes,
tear through the qualms
and uncertainties
that cloud you.

Now you rub its grit
between your fingers, now
you breathe this
grassy terrain

and it covers, no,
seals, no,

reclaims
the cracks and faults
in your shaken ground.

You are not a fragile
matter. You
are a height, no

an altitude, an elevation,
something higher,
a peak perhaps. Yes,
an imposing, irrepressible peak.
Yes, yes.

You Might Have Saved a Life

You might have saved a life tonight.

On impulse,
you might have looked
a faintly-known stranger
straight in the eyes
and caught sight of a life
waiting to ignite.

You might have reached in
and kindled it,

breathed wind
into this heat that burns
without flame,

flicked a spark
into a field of dry grass
and yelled "Live!"
or "Fire!" or "There is a gift
in these ashes that needs
to be scattered."

Tomorrow your stranger might
awaken alert and recalled,

they might set their Wild
Fire free and watch it spread
from sleeper to sleeper
until the world

shakes itself alive

and the murky sky starts
glowing.

You might have saved a life tonight.
You might have saved us all.

Unbecoming

I shall start this day
by engaging in an act
of unbecoming.

I shall begin
by awakening my ears
to the sound of
stretching.

Next,
I will peel away the voices
not of my making
and expose a self

that waits within.

I will lend it
what breath I have
for now.

Though the sun
has not yet risen,

I will bathe its skin
in light,

I shall allow
the universe to pour
into its most

minuscule cells
and spin inside.
With any luck

all this whirling
and light-tossing
will create a vastness

that will dislodge
the truest parts of me.

These pieces
shall swell; I shall

not stop this.

For some indefinite
period,

I may be enormous
and small
at the same time,

I shall strike a balance.

I shall untangle this self
from the day's
business

and feel something
in me float and
vibrate.

I will rise up
and make far more effort
to resist the dark.

A Beautiful Rain

You feel like a drought, yes,

but the soil does not crack
with your footsteps

nor do your bare feet
kick up dust.

Your breath does not draw
water from the dirt

or cause words
to crumble between
your teeth.

There is earth in you, yes,

but not sand. Not rock,
not desert, nothing sharp
or arid. Your edges

breathe and bend.
You pulse

in all the right
places.

There is a pool in your
heart, deep and sustaining.

Nothing has withered,
no one will drown here

or shrivel to bone.

There is storm
in your veins, yes,
but not a dry gust.

It is a beautiful rain, and
somewhere beneath it,

a field of wild grass and
tulips is spinning itself
to life.

The Wild Essential

Come close while I
undefine myself. I want
to peel away these labels
one letter at a time until
you see nothing but the
wild essential beneath.
Lift me from this box
then set me down in an
open field, let me tear
through the cattail and
burdock until sunup.
Unname me. Now bathe
me in light until I grow
my own meaning. Loosen
these concepts that limit
and bind, touch only
my truest skin.

Blue Moon

For John O'Donohue

While we await tonight's
blue moon,

let's toss out
these old maps and
help each other search
that space within,

close our eyes and
reach down deep

to claim the self
that breathes beneath
our uncertainty.

When the evening sun
pours through a spiral
of settling dust,

let's let it hit us
at such an angle

that all the rocks and
stones and soil in us shift

to reveal

a glowing landscape
that spills inside.

And as our true voices rise
with this rare moon,

let's look deliberately
at each other
and see a seamlessness
roll between,

touch,
and feel the infinite
within.

Morning Blend

By the time you rise
the grass will have dressed
itself in a light frost,
the sun will have washed
the night's stains from the sky,
the wind will have swept
the residue of fall
from the cracks in the
asphalt drive.
Sit back and savor
your French roast with
clear conscience,
the morning will manage
just fine with or without
your assistance.

Why I Received a Needs Improvement on My Last Employee Evaluation

Because the morning's first
streaks of orange produce
a rhythm within me

that I hear only when
my mind roams.

So I wake the dog,
and our six feet take
to the streets

and I offer my ideas
a region,

a span for them to swell
and float before the
neighborhood rises.

Because I stretch that space
between dark and day
so thin that the sky rips
and light pours in.

And there into that gap
I wander,

bathrobe under
winter coat,

forgetting that time

is not a midriff
and minutes can't expand
like a waistband at the
Panda City Buffet,

and there are only so many
simultaneous notions
I can travel

before I inch
towards rush hour.

How to Come Full Circle in Five Steps, More or Less

1. Return to the place
where you started
and feel hope rise
again like heat.

2. Though this spot
seemed so lost to you,
slip back seamlessly
into its loop. See how
its arc suits you,
how it fits and fills
the gaps and breaks,
all the empty inches
within you.

3. Now summon the day
the wind blew the musts
and shoulds, the can'ts
and won'ts away
from you. This is the
moment that marks
your re-beginning.

4. *Lean forward and
draw on the past.*
Make sure to send
yourself this message
over and again,
on a rolled slip affixed
to tired carrier pigeon

or through the mint
leaves that swirl
through your cup.

5. Spin three sixty and
soak in the stunning cuts
of light that bound
about this sight. Throw
open your eyes
and find yourself in this
open aired-space
changed, the same,
gloriously reclaimed.

Mind Monkeys

Hello monkeys,
any chance of dampening
your daytime havoc?
Toning down that screeching
chatter that echoes
between my ears?

Away you go swinging
across synapses,
hurling errands and
laundry lists. Hey pals,
quit stomping on memories,
flinging old fears around
with those wasted
bits of fruit.

Come chimp, let's take
a breather and sit
in stillness for a sec.
Won't you grant a high
strung *Homo sapiens*
a moment of mental
peace?

No? Maybe I can tempt
you with a little snack.
Let's break some bananas
together. Hey look,
isn't that a fig tree?
How about a lick of water
off a nice dewy leaf?

Now and Here

Watch this -

Now
we approach this oak,
red and dripping
with beauty.

First we forget
the wind
that will come to
undress these branches
when the cold drains
this landscape
of color,

then
the worries
that saturate our sleep
will dissolve
into this angle
of autumn light.

Here
we lose sight
of all things that hint
at earlier or
tomorrow
and slip ourselves
entirely
into this season.

See, *that*
is how these hills
recall us.

Sometimes Before It Storms

Sometimes before
it storms,

I pack a satchel
of peaches and
call myself Beloved.

I say such things as
"Beloved, you need
water" or "My beloved,
let's go to the sea."

I do not fret the mist,

it is a beach after all
and moisture is inherent
in the process. Besides,

a good peach always
pleases me.

I am content to let
the waves have their way
with my breath
until my lungs fall

and rise with their
rhythm.

I become
my own term of
endearment then

breathe myself
to life.

Dear, you
give me such grief
for disappearing
into the ocean,

but tell me,

without this,

how else could
I ever offer you
any fruit?

II

Your Biggest Thought

Below the minutia,
beneath those small
notions that whisper
"undoable,"

is that one thought

enormous and
bigger than you,

more massive

than this stretch of
night, this shadow
that swallows the moon.

You've felt it
swell before,
either upon waking
from a dream in the
early spring weeks,

or after one
too many cups
of fine Italian coffee.

It's the one that clamors
for your attention,
the one that's been

shouting "Yes to vast!
Yes to risk! Yes
to all things mammoth
and magnificent!"

Maybe it's time to quiet
the wee voices
that clutter your mind
and hear it out. Go on,
give it space, grow
huge with it.
Flourish.

Magnolias

Listen, I
need to say
just once in
this lifetime,
that when I
look at you
I see a
landscape,
alive and
soaked in
magnolias,
where I find
myself home
in fields I
have never
and always
known, to
which each
and every
turn, I
return.

A Kinder Suit

This year I want
for nothing but
fabric,

a kinder cloth
to shield me against
these blistering
doubts.

I wish to shed
the thoughts I wear
as hair shirts,

toss on layers
of linen and
soft knits,
silks and lenient
fibers,

run my fingers
along each thread
then feel my mind
breathe freely.

By next season
I will allow the wind
to loosen the beliefs
that limit
my movement,

I will reach,

feel forgiveness
wrap around me
like skin.

Threshold

You, my friend,
are a force,
the type of wind
that wipes the stars
clean.

Your thoughts
outshine the most
stunning
amalgamation of
elements that
embrace this earth.

So as you stand on
this threshold,
what makes you
crawl back
into that small
and sheltered crevice?
How do those
insignificant atoms
on the other side
bend your rock hard
will?

Listen friend, you are
a reckoning,
a gust that blows back
against the night.
So once and for all,

stop reading dread
into the hinges
and knob before you
and just step
through the door.

I Keep Checking My Samsung Galaxy
for Meaning

as if the universe
had fingertips
that were not far
too vast to type

or its messages
could swirl
through cloud
and silicon

then materialize
in my inbox;

as if I will
awaken
to a divine text

wrapped

in a glowing
bow of light
that says "Child,

all these
fraying ends

will someday tie
together"

while

the clues
I seek
burst into a

seamless display
of codes and
strings;

as if

everything
I need to know

isn't already
sitting in the
icy stillness

of this moonless
field

or swelling
in the gap
between

two breaths.

To the Moon

May these second thoughts
be launched into
deep space
then ditched
in a pocket
of pure silence.

There, where
nothing vibrates,
their babble will
finally fall mute,

they will stop tying
my mind in circles.

Let them drift towards
a band of unnamed stars,
be lost between
celestial bodies.

May they find their tanks
emptied of oxygen
before they finish
their last sentence.

Free as a Bear

There is a life out there
running amok with
your name on it.

Right now while
you are untangling
your frets from
your worries
and lacing
your options with
stones,

it is rummaging
through the foliage,
barefooted
and sweating,

recklessly
eating fistfuls
of berries.

See how it is
upending rocks
searching for your
presence?

Now it plants
itself onto the moss

and dips its toes
into a stream
of clear water;

it is whispering
sweet things
to the deer.

It is hoping
you will take
a wild moment
to come home
to yourself.

When it touches
the wind as
it tries to catch
the last of the tree
seeds,

its skin feels
only

what needs
to be known.

Lost Cause

Lost: One cause.

Last seen on a protest button
buried at the bottom
of a sewing basket
somewhere to the left of
a rusted thimble and
those seldom used spools
of fuchsia and teal.

 Previously took up company
with "End Apartheid" and
"No Nukes." May answer to
"World Peace" or "Save the
Spotted Eagle."

Possibly mislaid during
the great *"No Pants!" Toddler
Standoff* of February 2010
or somewhere between
the lines of that renegade
to-do list that picked up
momentum by the minute.

If found, kindly reconnect
owner to previous level
of commitment.

Rewards: Far-reaching.

Mending kit containing
thread in unlimited
shades of beige free
for the taking.

Lost and Found

Some mornings after you
wake up itchy,
you take to the freshly
cut fields and find
the self you once were
waiting by the bales
of hay.

It slips out from
time to time like this,
mostly on special days
like the leap year's
solstice or your
forty-seventh birthday.

Today you are wrapped
in dull grey fibers
while it is dons purple jellies
and a wrist full of rubber
bracelets in every shade
of the rainbow. It doesn't
have eczema.

You watch it run
its neon pink fingernails
along the cattail
and want to ask it burning
questions about 1984.

It reminds you that you lent
your long-lost Portuguese

fountain pen to
Shango Jablonski's sister
that Christmas, that

your dead brother's
letters are sitting
in a lockbox beneath
the closet floorboards,

that there's a silent
rock star in you and
you should be making
more art.

It is showing you how
the self you mislaid
is sitting within arm's reach
ready to rise through
the burdock;

fingers stretched,

skin clear,

body soaked
in color.

Make a Moment

My dear,
you have done all
that a shaken leaf
can do.

Please stop
beating your heart
for being
who you are,

and make a moment
for forgiveness.

When your breath
stops rushing between
lungs and lips,

reach into this
deepest fault
and lift that
unscarred part

who knows the sky
and light in you,

who breathes
your truest magic.

Dear, please
quiet those thoughts
that spin
your mind.

Now walk this self
into a sunlit room
and let it spill
your secrets.

III

Backwoods

Here is the answer to the question
you would never know to ask:

The space between the firs and
high grass where the mushrooms
rise silently under
fallen needles
is the place
where I come to need you
the only way I can make
that need known
in this lifetime,

quietly,

from the backwoods.

Silence Is the New Black

This morning
I will dress
myself neck
to toe
in silence
then step into
this field
to spin strands
of still cattail
into a quietly
patterned cloth.
I will wrap
this fabric
around my mind
like a turban
to swaddle
those fears that
snap branches.
The lists that
so sloppily spill
noise on my
synapses
will long last
be hushed,
I will muffle
the grievances
that thunder
under bone
and scalp.
Thread
by thread,

I will calm
this tangle of
chatter
until I hear
nothing but
heartbeat,
then detect,
rising into
that space
where wind
meets breath,
my voice.

After Cloud Cover

I am waiting for the day
to announce itself
in fiery streaks of
red and pink.

Instead, the night
simply drains itself
from the sky

offering
just enough light
to reveal a footpath
into the wild field.

Now slowly I see
where my feet
need to be

and exactly
what needs
to be done.

As I Brew My Morning Coffee

"If I miss you when I'm doing math,
can I sneak off into a corner and weep?"

"Can humans and dogs get married?
Can I marry a man with enormous muscles
so he can carry you around when you're
old and weak?"

"When I'm eighteen can I have ten kids?
Can you leave us the house and that
blue dress? Maybe all your clothes and
rings?"

"Will you come back every morning
to make their beds? Can you help me put
them in their car seats?"

"Can my kids sing Happy Birthday
at my grave when I'm dead?
Can they bury me a piece of cake?"

"Can they bury my body next to yours
so we can hold hands in the earth?"

"How does Grandpa live all alone?
How can he be so old and not know how
to juggle?"

"Will it hurt to have ten kids? Can you
do it for me? Should I marry a woman
so she can have the babies?"

"How old were you when your mommy
died? What if I get reborn and you can't
find me?"

"Where do you go to pee when you're
dead? Can I be a policegirl and also
make robots?"

"Can you wait until I'm a grandma
before you die?"

"Can dogs and robots get married?
What happens when one of them dies
or breaks?"

Watermarks

There are days
when I awaken
less solid than
otherwise.

Take yesterday
for instance,
when I slept
under an open
window and
the rain sank
through the
cracks in
my skin.
The rest of
the morning
your eyes
seeped from
the night's
dreams and
no matter how
hard I tried,
my heart
couldn't stop
leaking.

Watermarks
poured from
my fingers and
soaked my papers
in blue and

purple rings,
and by the time
I pulled myself
from that soggy
memory,
all the pools in me
had flooded.

Some days
I let the storm
receive me
like that. It's
how I keep this
life alive.

Headline News

This just in -
a local woman
in a town nowhere
near your house,
announced a personal matter
that pertains in no such
way, shape, or form
to anything having to do
with your particular
life situation.
We will share her story
for no compelling reason
and rerun it
every other segment
throughout the night
beginning at the top
of the hour.

In other late breaking
autumn news,
squirrels have been
pilfering acorns
while leaves
all over the northeast
have been taking
a tumultuous dive
towards the street.

Could this be a sign
of things to come

until the end
of November?

Stay with us,
please.

Anatomy of a Moment

Should I ever slip

and split open,

I am certain

that this stream

of light

that is

winding

its way

around you

would spill

from my skin

and I'd find

this rising

wind

woven through

tissue

and bands

of still

tendon

beneath.

Then deeper,

where bone

should be,

I no doubt

would see

cattail,

tall grass and

your hands

harvesting

a patch

of wild

tulips.

Warm Your One Sure Purpose

May this angle
of winter sun
warm your one
sure purpose,
may it toss
light upon your
certainty. May
the clarity of
this moment
pierce your
hesitation,
split the doubts
that taunt you
into a trillion
specks of dust.
May the last
bits of this
misgiving
be dispersed
over an icy
landscape,
cast with a
fistful of snow
back upwards
towards the sky.

I Carry a Field

Here is a sky of lost

      stars, here is the snow

thawing. Here is a

      moon swelling, here

the coyotes are

      howling a storm. Here

is a barn eaten

      by fire, there are

the torn trusses, here

      are the thin horses,

here are their manes

      matted with burs.

Here is the chestnut

      grove, there are the

bare deer bones,

      here, here, here

is the mountain.

    Now a wind is spilling,

now a wilderness

    is rising. All around is

an openness. Here, here,

    here a grain of earth.

An Open Letter to My True Self

I fed these ideas bricks,
allowed them to grow
fat and heavy with doubt,
render me motionless
while your voice rose
into the ether. You, who
sang of atmosphere,
who spun the wind
around you.

I'm ready to toss
these weights, silence
those unruly notions.
Help me trace your
whisper back home.
Let me hear this song
you've been humming,
teach me how to sing
of light.

Oxytocin

Sometimes I awaken
with an air rising in me
that sounds something
like wind climbing,

like silk winding,

like a cradlesong or hum
or some mysterious
harmony.

It had felt
like your voice
wrapping itself
around me
from the inside,

but maybe
it's been mine
trying to sing a love song
to myself.

Songbird

Baby, there's more
moving through you
than just the static
night.

You've got a symphony
swimming in those bones;
an act of wonder,
trying to work
its way out.

Stop mumbling like
your voice is nothing
but a still patch
of brambles and
weeds. Baby,

you're a songbird
and this day's sky
was meant for
your music.

Come, stretch
your neck and part
your lips, Love.
Let the morning
spill.

About the Author

Claudine Nash lives and writes in New York. She obtained a B.A. in English and Psychology from Wesleyan University and later went on to obtain two master's degrees and a Ph.D. in Psychology from Connecticut College and St. John's University. Heavily influenced by her background in psychology, her poetry frequently delves into such topics as loss, healing and the liberation of releasing the past. Her most recent writings have focused on the power of connecting to our authentic selves and finding our true inner voice.

Her previous collections include her full-length poetry book *Parts per Trillion (*Aldrich Press, 2016) and her chapbook *The Problem with Loving Ghosts* (Finishing Line Press, 2014). She also edited the collection *In So Many Words: Interviews and Poetry from Today's Poets* (Madness Muse Press, 2016) with Adam Levon Brown.

Claudine's poetry has earned numerous literary distinctions including Pushcart Prize nominations and prizes from such publications as *Eye on Life Magazine, The Song Is...,Thirty West Publishing House, Avalon Literary Review* and *Lady Chaos Press.* Internationally published, her poems have appeared in a wide range of magazines and anthologies including *Asimov's Science Fiction, BlazeVOX, Cloudbank, Haight Ashbury Literary Journal* and *Dime Show Review* amongst others.

In addition to appearing in print form, Claudine's poetry has also been integrated into a number of other art forms. As one of the Grand Prize Winners of the 24th Annual Artists Embassy International's Dancing Poetry Contest, her poem "How to Come Full Circle in Five Steps, More or Less" was choreographed and performed by Natica Angilly's Poetic Dance Theater Company in San Francisco in 2017. Her poetry has also been put to music by singer-songwriter Madalyn Barbero Jordan and displayed in numerous gallery exhibits within the paintings and photography of artist Carlos Monteagudo.

www.ingramcontent.com/pod-product-compliance
Lightning Source LLC
La Vergne TN
LVHW020100090426
835510LV00040B/2668